MW00768611

Nita Mehta's

Eggless Desserts

100% Vegetarian

Nita Mehta

B.Sc. (Home Science), M.Sc. (Food and Nutrition), Gold Medalist

Tanya Mehta

SNAB
Publishers Pvt Ltd

Nita Mehta's **Eggless Desserts**

© Copyright 2003 **SNAB** Publishers Pvt Ltd

WORLD RIGHTS RESERVED. The contents—all recipes, photographs and drawings are original and copyrighted. No portion of this book shall be reproduced, stored in a retrieval system or transmitted by any means, electronic, mechanical, photocopying, recording or otherwise, without the written permission of the publishers.

While every precaution is taken in the preparation of this book, the publisher and the author assume no responsibility for errors or omissions. Neither is any liability assumed for damages resulting from the use of information contained herein.

TRADEMARKS ACKNOWLEDGED. Trademarks used, if any, are acknowledged as trademarks of their respective owners. These are used as reference only and no trademark infringement is intended upon.

First Edition 2003
ISBN 81-7869-049-7

Food Styling and Photography: **SNAB**

Layout and laser typesetting :

National Information
Technology Academy
3A/3, Asaf Ali Road
N.I.T.A. New Delhi-110002
☎ 23252948

Published by :

SNAB
Publishers Pvt. Ltd.
3A/3 Asaf Ali Road,
New Delhi - 110002
Tel: 23252948, 23250091
Telefax:91-11-23250091

Editorial and Marketing office:
E-348, Greater Kailash-II, N.Delhi-48
*Fax:*91-11-26235218 *Tel:*91-11-26214011, 26238727
E-Mail: nitamehta@email.com
snab@snabindia.com
*Website:*http://www.nitamehta.com
Website: http://www.snabindia.com

Distributed by :
THE VARIETY BOOK DEPOT
A.V.G. Bhavan, M 3 Con Circus,
New Delhi - 110 001
Tel : 23417175, 23412567; Fax : 23415335

Printed by :
INTERNATIONAL PRINT-O-PAC LIMITED

Rs. 89/-

Introduction

H ere is a treasury of elegant sweet dishes including classic desserts as well as a good selection of the new ones. Your friends will look forward to your invitations to dinner and vote you the world's greatest dessert maker!

Indulge yourself with chocolate desserts, cool off with delicious home made ice creams and ice cream desserts or finish a perfect meal with a perfect cheese cake! There are hot pudding and pies which seem so difficult to make, but you will be surprised to see how easy these are once you follow the recipe step by step. An array of delectable egg free cakes and gateaux laced with fruits and drenched in sauces shall be a great treat for any occasion. The classic soufflés and mousses have been created bringing out new flavours. Fresh fruits have been used to prepare pretty coloured and exotic flavoured soufflés and mousses. Even when not on a diet, the low calorie desserts included in the book will be more than welcome to you, your friends and family.

I believe my research on desserts has been a fruitful attempt to satisfy my readers.

Nita Mehta

ABOUT THE RECIPES

WHAT'S IN A CUP?

INDIAN CUP
1 teacup = 200 ml liquid
AMERICAN CUP
1 cup = 240 ml liquid (8 oz.)
The recipes in this book were tested with the Indian teacup which holds 200 ml liquid.

Contents

Ice Cream 'n' Icecream Desserts   25

Fruity Cappuccino Ice Cream Cake   26

Black Currant Ice Cream   29

Quick Ice Cream Trifle   30

Pineapple Yogurt Ice Cream   32

Cookies & Cream   34

Cakes & Gateaux   35

Excess Chocolate Ruffle   36

Brownie with Toffee Sauce   40

Wild Strawberry Chocolate Cake   42

Eggless Vanilla Cake   44

Eggless Chocolate Cake   45

Cherry Choco Biscuit Cake   46

Fresh Fruit Gateau   49

Lattice Strawberry Gateau   51

Orange Chiffon Cake with Orange Honey Sauce   54

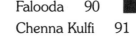

Cheese Cakes

China Grass (Agar agar) as a Setting Agent for Cheese cakes

China Grass is a sea weed and absolutely vegetarian. It needs to be broken into smaller pieces and soaked in a liquid, generally water, for 5 minutes to soften as shown in the picture. After soaking, heat gently, stirring continuously on low heat, to melt. *The hot melted agar agar should be added immediately into the dessert mix, and the dessert mix should be stirred continuously while*

the china grass is being added. If the china grass mixture solidifies before it can be added, you can reheat and melt it on low heat again. China grass sets very easily and does not need a cold temperature to set it, so sometimes the liquid sets before it is added to the dessert mixture. *The dessert mixture also should be warm or atleast at room temperature and never cold. If melted china grass is added to a cold mixture it sets as tiny rubber like pieces and does not blend with the dessert mixture well. The dessert also then does not set properly.*

Striped Chocolate Cheese Cake

A beautiful white and chocolate striped cheese cake. Only the base is baked whereas the cheese cake is set in the refrigerator.

Serves 12

BISCUIT BASE
100 gms Marie biscuits (1 small pack)
½ cup melted butter
2 tbsp milk

CHEESE CAKE
4½ cups curd - hang for 2 hours in a thin muslin cloth
125 gm butter (¾ cup) - softened (at room temperature)
1¾ cups powdered sugar
1½ packets (15 gm) of china grass
2 tsp lemon juice
1 slab (of 40 gm) chocolate, preferably cooking or dark chocolate - at room temperature

Step 1

1. Place the biscuits in a plastic bag and crush the biscuits with a rolling pin.
2. Mix in melted butter with finger tips and add 2 tbsp milk. Mix well.
3. Put at the base of an 8" loose bottomed cake tin or a flat glass dish. Press with the back of a small steel bowl.

Step 3

4. Bake in a pre-heated oven at 180°C/350°F for 10 minutes.
5. Hang the curd for 2 hours in a muslin cloth.
6. Beat butter (it should not be cold) till smooth. Add hung curd and sugar. Beat well till smooth.
7. Break china grass into small pieces and put in a heavy bottom pan. Pour 2 cups water on it and leave for 5 minutes to soften. Stir on very low heat, for 5-6 minutes till it melts completely. Do not let it boil.
8. Gradually add **hot china grass** solution into curd mixture, **stirring well with the other hand immediately**, after each addition. Beat well. Check sugar. Add more depending on the sourness of the curd.

9. Divide the mixture into two parts.

Step 10

10. Cut the chocolate into small pieces.
11. Add ¼ cup water to the chocolate and keep in a heavy bottomed pan on very low heat, stirring until melted properly. Add ½ of the melted chocolate to one cheese cake mixture, keeping the other mixture white.
12. Pour the chocolate curd mixture on the biscuit base in the tin. Keep the white mixture aside.
13. Chill chocolate cheese cake for 10 minutes in the freezer to firm up.

Step 14

14. Remove from freezer. Pour remaining white mixture (whip it if it sets) on top of the chocolate mixture and now chill in the refrigerator. (Do not keep in the freezer).
15. After 1 hour, when the top layer of the cheese cake is set, pour the left over melted chocolate over the cheese cake. Serve after 3-4 hours or after it is set.

Black Grape Cheese Cake

Delicious cheese cake, with a beautiful purple shade. An eye pleasing dessert.

Serves 8

BASE

22 chocolate chip biscuits, 7 tbsp melted butter
7-8" diameter loose bottom cake tin

CHEESE CAKE

500 gm cream, 1 cup powdered sugar, 5 level tbsp cheese spread
1½ packets (15 gm) china grass
a drop of strawberry pink colour, optional

BLACK GRAPE SAUCE

200 gm (1½ cups grapes), 5 tbsp sugar, 1 cup water, 4 tsp lemon juice

TOPPING

2-3 tbsp black grape jam or mixed fruit jam, 2 biscuits - crushed roughly
6-8 black grapes, 1 tsp powdered sugar to dust

1. Grind the chocolate chip biscuits in grinder. Add melted butter and mix well. Spread at the bottom of the flat glass dish or a loose bottom tin. Press well with the back of a steel bowl and keep in the fridge to set.
2. Beat cream with sugar and cheese spread till slightly thick and fluffy. Keep aside and not in the fridge.
3. For the grape sauce, boil all ingredients together. Simmer for 10 minutes till grapes turn soft. Keep mashing the grapes in-between. (It should not be thick). Remove from fire. Cover and keep aside.
4. Break china grass into small pieces and put in a pan. Pour 2 cups water on it and leave for 5 minutes to soften. Stir on low heat, for 5-6 minutes till it melts completely. Do not let it boil.
5. Strain hot china grass solution into the **hot grape mixture**, stirring well with the other hand. Keep aside till it cools to room temperature.
6. Add the grape mixture to the cream and beat well to mix properly. Add colour if required. Check sugar and add more if required.
7. Pour over the biscuit crust and keep in the fridge for 3-4 hours to set.
8. Decorate with a border of biscuits crumbs. Beat 2-3 tbsp jam & spread in the centre. Arrange grapes on the jam and sprinkle powdered sugar.

Glazed Sesame Mango Cheese Cake

Picture on page 1   *Serves 8*

CRUST
1 packet (12) digestive biscuits (Britannia), 3 tbsp melted butter, 1 tbsp milk

CHEESE CAKE
1 cup fresh curd - hang for 15-20 minutes
200 gm paneer - grated finely, 2 tbsp cheese spread
1 large mango - pureed in a mixer (1 cup), (you can use tinned mangoes too!)
1 packet (10 gm) china grass , ¾ cup powdered sugar, or to taste
½ tsp vanilla essence, a drop of yellow colour, optional

GLAZE SESAME TOPPING
1 cup mango fruity or any mango drink, 1 tbsp sugar, 1 tbsp cornflour
¼ tsp butter, pinch black sesame seeds (kale til) - roasted on a tawa for 1-2 min

1. For the crust, crush biscuits with a rolling pin (belan) to get coarse biscuit crumbs as shown on page 12. Add butter and mix. Add milk. Mix well. Press the mixture at the bottom of a 7" loose bottom tin or a

      flat round dish as shown on page 12. Keep in the freezer compartment of the fridge for 15 minutes to set.

2. In a mixer, put hung curd, paneer and cheese spread. Churn, scraping sides in between, till the mixture becomes smooth. Remove to a pan.

3. Heat mango puree on low heat till just warm. Cover and keep aside.

4. Break china grass into small pieces and put in a pan. Pour 1¼ cups water on it and leave for 5 minutes to soften. Stir on low heat, for 5-6 minutes till it melts completely. Do not let it boil.

5. Add hot china grass solution in small amounts into the **warm** mango puree, stirring well with the other hand.

6. Add mango puree to the curd-paneer mixture and beat well.

7. Add sugar. Add more if required. Add essence and colour.

8. Pour over the set biscuit crust. Place in the fridge to set for 2-3 hours.

9. For the glaze, mix juice, cornflour and sugar in a pan. Keep on fire, stirring continuously till it turns thick and starts to coat the spoon. Add butter. Remove from fire. Let it cool to room temperature. Pour the glaze on the cheese cake. Sprinkle some toasted black sesame seeds on the set cheese cake and refrigerate till serving time.

Lemon Cheese Cake

Picture on facing page   Serves 4-5

250 gm (1¼ cups) fresh cream, ½ tin (¾ cup) condensed milk - cold
¼ cup lemon juice (juice of 4 lemons), rind of 1 lemon (1 tbsp), read step 4
a pinch or a few drops yellow colour

BASE
1 packet (10) good day biscuits, 4 tbsp (50 gm) butter - melted

1. Keep the cream in a bowl and chill for 10 minutes in the freezer.
2. To prepare the base, pre-heat oven to 180°C. Break good day biscuits into pieces and put in a polythene. Crush to a coarse powder with a rolling pin. Do not make them too fine. Put them in a bowl. Melt butter and add 4 tbsp melted butter to the biscuit crumbs. Mix well.
3. Spread crumbs in a small loose bottomed pie dish or a serving dish, (a small square borosil dish in fine). Press well. Bake at 180°C for 10 minutes. Remove from oven and cool.
4. Wash & grate 1 lemon with the peel gently on the grater to get lemon rind. Do not apply pressure and see that the white pith beneath the

Contd...

lemon peel is not grated along with the yellow rind. The white pith is bitter!

5. Take out ¼ cup lemon juice. Add the lemon rind to it. Empty ½ tin of cold condensed milk (keep condensed milk in fridge) into a bowl. Add lemon juice and beat well. The condensed milk turns thick on whipping. Keep in the fridge.

Step 4

6. Beat chilled cream in the chilled bowl with an electric egg beater (electric hand mixer) till soft peaks are formed. After soft peaks are ready, beat gently with a spoon till firm peaks are formed. Beat carefully in a cool place or over ice, taking care not to beat vigorously. The cream should remain smooth and not turn buttery or granular. Put about ½ cup cream in an icing bag for decoration and keep in the fridge.

7. Add half of the thickened condensed milk to the cream in the bowl. Fold condensed milk gently into the cream to mix well. Fold in the left over condensed milk too. Add enough colour to get a nice yellow colour.

8. Pour the cream mix over the cooled biscuit base in the dish. Keep in the fridge for at least 3 hours to set. To serve, cut into pieces.

◁ *Quick Ice Cream Triffle: Recipe on page 30*

Fresh Strawberry Cheese Cake

Serves 8-10

5 cups thick curd - hang for ½ hour in a thin muslin cloth
250 gm (1½ cups) fresh cream
2 tbsp cheese spread
¾ cup powdered sugar, or to taste
200 gm strawberries - pureed in a mixer (1½ cups), see note
1½ packets (15 gm) china grass

BASE

a sponge cake, see note
4-5 tbsp strawberry crush or jam - beat well to make it smooth
2-3 tbsp cold milk

GARNISH

4-5 fresh strawberries - sliced thinly
1 tbsp powdered sugar

1. Break china grass into small pieces and put in a pan. Pour 2 cups water on it and leave for 5 minutes to soften. Keep aside.
2. Beat cream with sugar till slightly fluffy but still thin.
3. Beat hung curd till smooth. Add cheese spread and whip till smooth.
4. Mix the whipped cream and curd mixture.
5. Stir softened china grass on low heat, for 5-6 minutes till it melts completely.
6. Warm the puree on low heat. Add the hot china grass solution into the **warmed strawberry puree**, stirring well with the other hand.
7. Add the strawberry mixture to the curd-cream mixture and beat well to mix properly. Add colour if required and mix well to get a nice pink colour. Check sugar, add more powdered sugar if required, depending on the sourness of the curd and fruit.
8. Keep aside for 10-20 minutes, or till slightly thick, but do not let it set.
9. Meanwhile, cut a ½" thick slice from the bottom of the sponge cake. Place the cake at the bottom of a loose bottomed flan tin or a flat glass dish, such as to cover the base. Press well.

Contd...

10. Sprinkle some cold milk on the cake. Spread 3-4 tbsp crush or jam on it and keep in the fridge to chill.

11. When the curd-cream mixture becomes slightly thick, beat it till smooth and pour over the cake in the flan tin. Keep in the fridge for at least 4-6 hours or till set.

12. To decorate, cut 4-5 fresh strawberries into thin slices and sprinkle 1 tbsp powdered sugar. Mix gently and cover the top completely with strawberry slices.

Note:

◆ If fresh strawberries are not available, you can use ½ cup strawberry crush mixed with ½ cup hot boiling water instead. Since the crush has sugar in it, reduce the sugar to 8 tbsp instead of ¾ cup. Warm the crush mixture before adding china grass.

◆ If you do not want to use a sponge cake, make a biscuit crust as given for black grape cheese cake.

Ice Cream
'n'
Icecream Desserts

Fruity Cappuccino Ice Cream Cake

Serves 8

7" vanilla cake flavoured with rind of 1 lemon, see page 44 (½ quantity)
500 gm cappuccino (Amul ice cream) or chocolate chip ice cream
½ cup milk mixed with 2 tbsp chocolate sauce

FRUITY SAUCE
1 cup black grapes, ¼ cup sugar, ½ cup water

FRUITY FILLING
1 cup grapes - desseded, if required, 1 tsp butter, ¼ cup water
4 tbsp strawberry crush or 2 tbsp strawberry jam

DECORATION (OPTIONAL)
100 gm whipped cream, chocolate thins or nutties, chocolate sprinklers, mint
some ready-made chocolate sauce

1. Make vanilla cake batter using half tin of milk maid, as given on page 44. Make all the other ingredients half also to get a smaller cake. Add lemon rind to the cake batter. To get lemon rind, wash and grate

1 lemon with peel gently on the grater. Do not apply pressure and see that the white pith beneath the lemon peel is not grated along with yellow rind. The white pith is bitter!

Step 1

2. For the fruity sauce, place sugar, water and stir on fire till sugar dissolves. Add grapes & cook, mashing, till soft for about 5 minutes. Cool. Strain to get a thin fruit sauce.

3. For filling, heat butter in a pan. Add grapes, stir and add strawberry crush & water. Simmer for 2 min. Mash slightly. Remove from fire.

4. To assemble, cut cake into half. Pour sauce on both pieces on the cut surface and spread. Spread 2-3 tbsp ice cream on a piece and invert the other piece of cake on it. Keep aside.

5. Clean the tin. In the same empty cake tin, spread about 2" thick ice cream layer.

6. Swirl about ½ cup chocolate sauce or chocolate syrup on ice cream.

7. Top with grape filling.

Contd...

8. Place the cake on the grape filling. Press cake well. Some ice cream will come up from the sides.

9. Mix ½ cup cold milk with 2-3 tbsp chocolate syrup and pour on the cake to keep it moist. Cover with wrap and put in the freezer for 3-4 hours to set.

10. 2-3 hours before serving invert the ice cream cake on the serving plate, such that you get the ice cream on top. Loosen the sides first and rub the back of the tin with a hot towel or hands after inverting, if it is difficult to unmould. You can dip the towel in hot water and squeeze or warm it in a microwave.

11. After the cake is inverted on the plate, sprinkle chocolate sprinklers or grate some chocolate on the ice cream which is now on the top. Squeeze chocolate sauce on the edges all around so that some flows on the sides too. Decorate with swirls of whipped cream and a sprig of mint. Arrange chocolate thins or nutties or cherries on the whipped cream. Cover loosely with wrap. Freeze till serving time.

Black Currant Ice Cream

Serves 6-8

250 gm black grapes, 7 tbsp sugar, ½ packet china grass
500 gm fresh cream, 12 tbsp powdered sugar
2 tbsp black raisins (kali kishmish) - soaked in 1 tbsp rum or brandy

1. Cook grapes with 4 tbsp water and 7 tbsp sugar over low heat, for about 10 minutes. When grapes are fully softened, remove from the heat and allow to cool. Blend to a pulp in a mixer. Strain if there are seeds. Heat on fire till about to boil. Cover and keep aside.
2. Break china grass into small pieces and put in a pan. Pour ¾ cup water on it and leave for 5 minutes to soften. Stir on low heat, for 5-6 minutes till it melts completely.
3. Add hot china grass solution into the **hot grape mixture**, stirring well with the other hand. Mix well and keep aside.
4. Beat cream and sugar until thick but pouring consistency.
5. Add cream to the grapes and beat well. Add raisins along with rum.
6. Pour mixture into an ice cream box. Freeze overnight or till firm.

Quick Ice Cream Trifle

A quick fix-up dessert, sure to get you a lot of appreciation.

Picture on page 20   *Serves 8*

3-4 black forest pastries or coffee pastries or any other
1 tin mixed fruit (fruit cocktail tin) or 2 cups chopped fresh fruits
¼ tsp cinnamon powder (dalchini powder)
1 pack (500 ml) vanilla ice cream
4-5 tbsp chocolate sauce to top
a few almonds - cut into thin long pieces

1. If using fresh fruits, boil ¾ cup water with ¼ cup sugar and juice of ½ lemon. Add hard fruits like apple or pears and bring to a boil. Remove from fire and strain after 5 minutes. Keep syrup aside. Add soft fruits like grapes, strawberries to the cooled syrup. Do not boil soft fruits. This step is not to be done, if using tinned fruits.
2. Cut the pastry into slices, reserving cherries for the top. Place them in a shallow serving dish covering the bottom of the dish. Spread cream of the pastries evenly all over with a spoon.

3. Soak pastries with ½ cup of fruit syrup so that it becomes moist.
4. Drain the fruits. Spread the fruits on the pastries.
5. Sprinkle cinnamon powder on the fruits. Cover and keep in the fridge till serving time.
6. At serving time, top the fruit with scoops of ice cream, 1 scoop for each person and a few extra ones for the people with hearty appetites!
7. Squeeze a few circles within circle, (like jalebis) of chocolate sauce on the ice cream.
8. Decorate with some almonds and reserved cherries. Serve immediately.

Pineapple Yogurt Ice Cream

Hung curd is used instead of cream for preparing the ice cream.

Serves 10

5 cups full-cream milk
6 tbsp skimmed milk powder
½ cup sugar
½ packet (5 gm) china grass soaked in ¾ cup water
½ kg (2½ cups) curd prepared from full-cream milk
5 tbsp powdered sugar, few drops yellow colour
2 tsp pineapple essence, 1 tsp vanilla essence
1 pineapple slice (tinned) - cut into fine pieces, optional

1. Dissolve milk powder in ½ cup warm milk and keep aside.
2. Strain the milk powder paste into the leftover 4½ cups milk.
3. Add sugar. Boil milk, stirring occasionally.
4. Keep on medium flame for 25 minutes after the first boil. Adjust the flame so as to keep the milk boiling slowly all the time. Stir frequently

to prevent the milk from boiling over.

5. Break china grass into small pieces and put in a pan. Pour ½ cup water on it and leave for 5 minutes to soften. Stir on low heat, for 2-3 minutes till it melts completely.

6. After the milk has been on fire for 25 minutes, remove from fire. Add the hot china grass solution into the **hot milk**, stirring continuously. Mix well and return to fire. Cook for 1 minute more on very low heat. Do not let it boil. Remove from fire. Cool. Cover well and freeze for 4-5 hours or overnight, or till set.

7. When the milk has frozen, hang the curd in a muslin cloth for ½ hour. Squeeze gently to remove any excess liquid.

8. Beat hung curd with sugar and both the essences till smooth.

9. Cut frozen milk into small pieces. Beat till fluffy. Mix the hung curd in it. Add colour. Mix.

10. Transfer to an ice cream box. Squeeze pineapple pieces well and sprinkle on the ice cream. Mix gently. Cover nicely with a cling wrap first and then with the lid of the box and freeze till firm.

Cookies & Cream

A simple vanilla ice cream turned special!

Serves 12

1 family brick vanilla ice cream - ready-made
1 packet chocolate chip cookies (Britannia), 12 pieces

1. Roughly break the cookies into small pieces. Keep in the freezer for ½ hour to harden.
2. Beat the vanilla ice cream till soft with an electric hand beater.
3. Spread half of the ice cream in an ice cream box.
4. Sprinkle half of the cookie pieces on the ice cream.
5. Repeat ice cream and biscuit layer again. Freeze till firm. Unmould and serve after 5-6 hours.
6. Serve the ice cream topped with a cookie half.

Cakes & Gateaux

Excess Chocolate Ruffle

Picture on facing page   *Serves 6-8*

CHOCOLATE CAKE
1 cup maida (flour), ½ cup cornflour, ¼ cup cocoa
1½ tsp baking powder, ¾ tsp soda-bi-carb
¾ cup white butter (75-80 gm), ¾ cup powdered sugar
1 cup milk, ½ tsp vanilla essence
20 gm dark chocolate or milk chocolate mixed with 4 tbsp milk
a ring tin for baking

CHOCOLATE RUFFLES
½ cup yellow butter - softened, 1 cup icing sugar - sifted
½ cup cocoa, 2-3 tbsp hot water

TO SOAK
1 cup mixed fruit juice or orange juice

GARNISH
10-15 almonds - blanched (peel removed by soaking) & split

1. Sift flour, cornflour, cocoa, baking powder and soda-bi-carb.
2. Beat butter& sugar till fluffy. Add flour mix and 1 cup milk. Mix well.
3. Cut chocolate into small pieces. Melt with 4 tbsp milk in a heavy bottomed kadhai on very low heat.
4. Add melted chocolate and essence to the cake batter. Beat till fluffy.
5. Bake in a greased ring cake tin at 180°C for 30-35 minutes. Remove from oven and let it cool.
6. After the cake cools down, remove from tin and slice into 2 round halves. Soak cut surface of both pieces with orange juice.
7. For the ruffle icing, put cocoa in a bowl. Pour hot water on it and mix well to get a dark paste. Add butter and mix well. Add sifted icing sugar and beat well with a beater for 2-3 minutes till the icing is fluffy.
8. Place one piece of the cake in a serving platter. Spread 2 tbsp icing on it and invert the second piece of cake on it.
9. Spread left over icing on the cake. Keep in the fridge to set for 15 min.
10. Draw lines with a fork, starting from the bottom of the cake till the top to give it a ruffled look. Decorate with a row of almonds. Keep in the fridge till the time of serving. Serve with vanilla ice cream if you like.

◁ *Lattice Strawberry Gateau : Recipe on page 51*

Brownie with Toffee Sauce

Picture on page 2   *Makes 4-6*

1 cup flour (maida)
½ cup cocoa
½ cup chopped walnuts
1 cup curd (use fresh curd)
¾ cup ordinary sugar
1½ tsp baking powder
½ tsp soda bicarb (mitha soda)
½ cup oil
1 tsp vanilla essence

TOFFEE SAUCE
1½ tbsp butter - softened
4 tbsp jaggery (powdered gur)
4-6 tbsp fresh cream
2 tbsp roughly chopped walnuts

1. Mix sugar and curd well. Stir till sugar dissolves completely.
2. Add baking powder and soda. Mix well. Keep aside for 3-4 minutes till bubbles start to appear.
3. Sieve the flour and cocoa. Mix walnuts with the flour. Keep aside.
4. Add oil to the curd mixture. Add essence. Mix well.
5. Lastly add the flour and mix well to get a thick but soft batter. Add a little more curd if the batter appears too thick and hard.
6. Transfer the mixture into a greased 7" square baking tin.
7. Bake in a preheated oven at 210°C for 10 minutes. Reduce heat to 150°C and bake further for 20-25 minutes or until done. Test with a knife to see that it comes out clean. Remove from oven after 5 minutes.
8. Let the cake cool in the tin for 10 minutes and then remove from tin. Cut into triangular or square pieces.
9. For the sauce, heat butter in a small thick bottomed sauce pan on medium heat. Add the jaggery. Cook for 1 minute till the mixture is frothy. Remove from heat. Add the cream. Return to low heat. Stir for a few seconds till well blended. Do not bring to a boil. Add the walnuts.
10. Remove from fire and pour over the brownies.

Wild Strawberry Chocolate Cake

Picture on cover   *Serves 8*

1 cup maida (flour), ½ cup cornflour, ¼ cup cocoa
1½ tsp baking powder, ¾ tsp soda-bi-carb
¾ cup white butter (75-80 gm), ¾ cup powdered sugar
1 cup milk, ½ tsp vanilla essence
20 gm dark chocolate or milk chocolate mixed with 4 tbsp milk

GLAZED STRAWBERRIES
200 gm (1 packet) strawberries - cut into slices, 4 tbsp sugar

SOAKING SYRUP
¾ cup water, 1½ tbsp sugar, 1 tsp coffee, 1 tsp vanilla essence
½ cup chocolate sauce

1. Sift flour, cornflour, cocoa, baking powder and soda-bi-carb.
2. Beat butter & sugar till fluffy. Add flour mixture and 1 cup milk. Mix.
3. Cut chocolate into small pieces. Melt with 4 tbsp milk in a heavy

bottomed kadhai on very low heat.

4. Add melted chocolate and essence to the cake batter. Beat till fluffy.

5. Bake in a greased 7-8" diameter cake tin at 180°C for 30-35 minutes. Remove from oven and let it cool.

6. For the strawberries, mix ¼ cup water and 4 tbsp sugar in a pan. Stirring continuously, cook on low heat till sugar melts. Cook further for 2 minutes. Remove from fire. After it cools, add strawberry slices to the sugar syrup and stir gently for a few seconds till well coated and glazed. Remove the glazed strawberries to a plate with a slotted spoon, leaving the syrup behind in the pan.

7. For the soaking syrup, boil water and sugar. Add coffee and remove from fire. Add essence. Let it cool down.

8. Place the cake in a serving platter with the bottom side on top. Soak it with coffee syrup till very moist. Pour chocolate sauce on it. Spread to cover the top nicely till the edges. Let it drip from the sides.

9. Arrange slices of strawberry on the cake, starting from the outer edge. Place the next row slightly overlapping the first. Make the centre slices sit a little upright. Keep in the refrigerator. Cut into wedges to serve.

Eggless Vanilla Cake

Makes about 1¼ kg, serves 12-16, a big baking tin of 11-12" diameter is required, so make half the quantity if you have a small cake tin for baking.

1 tin (400 gm) condensed milk (milk-maid)
1½ cups (300 ml) milk
1¼ cups (180 gm) white butter
3 tbsp powdered sugar
250 gms (2½ cups) maida (plain flour)
1 tsp level soda-bi-carb, 2 tsp level baking powder
2 tsp vanilla essence

1. Preheat oven to 150°C for 10 minutes.
2. Sift maida with soda-bi-carb and baking powder. Keep aside.
3. Mix sugar and butter in a big pan. Beat till very fluffy and light.
4. Add milk-maid. Beat well to mix.
5. Add milk. Mix well. Add essence.
6. Add the maida gradually beating well after each addition.

7. Beat well for 3-4 minutes till the mixture is smooth and light and of a soft dropping consistency.
8. Grease and dust a big round cake tin. Put the cake batter in it.
9. Smoothen the top, pushing the mixture backwards from the centre to make a slight depression in the centre. This prevents the forming of a peak!
10. Bake for 50-60 minutes in a pre-heated oven at 150°C. Check with a knife at the highest point of the cake. Remove from oven after 5 minutes.
11. Wait for another 5-10 minutes before removing from the tin on to the wire rack. Let it cool down and then put it back in the tin in which it was baked. Cover well with a plastic wrap and keep outside the fridge.

Eggless Chocolate Cake

Follow the same method as for vanilla cake, but instead of 2½ cups maida, use 2 cups maida plus ½ cup cocoa powder. Sift the cocoa powder also with the maida. Reduce the essence to 1 tsp.

Cherry Choco Biscuit Cake

Picture on facing page   *Serves 4*

200 gms Marie biscuits (1 large packet)
1 cup chocolate sauce (ready-made), 2½ tbsp cream
10-15 blanched (peel removed by soaking in hot water) & chopped almonds
1 tbsp kishmish (raisins), ¼ cup (10-12) glace cherries - chopped finely

1. Line a cake tin or a small square borosil dish with a large piece of aluminium foil, such that the foil is extra on all sides. Press foil carefully.
2. Break the biscuits into tiny pieces and put them into a shallow bowl. Add most of the cherries, keeping aside some for the top.
3. Add the raisins and almonds also to the biscuit mixture.
4. Add cream and chocolate sauce into the biscuit mixture. Mix everything well. Put the mixture into the tin on the foil and level it with a spoon.
5. Press left over cherries on top. Cover cake with foil from all sides. Press it down firmly. Put the cake in the fridge for about 2 hours until it sets. Lift it out of the tin with the help of foil. Peel off the foil. Serve.

Fresh Fruit Gateau

Serves 8   *Picture on opposite page*

an eggless vanilla cake (page 44) - cut cake into 2 or 3 round halves
350 gms fresh cream - keep in the freezer for only 10 min before beating, to chill
7 tbsp powdered sugar, 1 tsp vanilla essence, 1 tsp lemon juice (lemon juice
prevents curdling of cream!), 3 tbsp strawberry jam or crush, 1 cup orange juice
fresh fruits of different colours - strawberries, chiku or kiwi, grapes or cherries

GLAZE
¼ cup sugar, ¼ cup water
½ tsp butter
1 tsp cornflour

1. Whip chilled cream in a cold pan with powdered sugar, essence &
   lemon juice on ice till it can stand in firm peaks.
2. Fill some whipped cream in the icing gun. Keep whipped cream which
   is in the pan and the gun in the refrigerator.
3. Soak each piece of cake with orange juice on the cut surface.

Contd...

4. Slice the fruit for topping and cut the not so neat pieces into tiny cubes to get about ½ cup of chopped fruit.

5. Place one piece of cake (top side down) on the serving plate. Put 2-3 tbsp heaped cream and spread gently. Spread some chopped fruit.

6. Apply crush or jam on the second piece of cake and invert on the fruits. Press. Repeat if there are 3 pieces of cake.

7. Cover the final piece of cake with cream on the top and sides. Cut grapes into halves and press on the sides on the cream. Pipe a cream border on the edges.

8. Decorate with fresh fruits. Start by arranging strawberries on the cuter border. Half the kiwi or chiku slices and fix a row of them at the ends of strawberries, slightly overlapping each other, keeping them a little upright by making them rest on the strawberries. Fix another row in the same way around it. Arrange grapes or cherries in the centre.

9. For the glaze, boil sugar, water and cornflour together for 2-3 minutes till a thin glaze is ready. Add butter. Remove from heat. Let it cool down. Spoon or brush the glaze on the arranged fruits. Refrigerate till the time of serving.

Lattice Strawberry Gateau

Serves 6-7   *Picture on page 38*

1 vanilla sponge cake of 11-12" diameter - page 44

GLAZED STRAWBERRIES
250 gm (1 packet) strawberries
4 tbsp sugar

SOAKING SYRUP
2 tsp cornflour dissolved in ½ cup water
1 tbsp brandy or rum or 1 tsp strawberry essence

WHIPPED CREAM
400 gm cream, 1 tsp lemon juice (lemon juice prevents curdling of cream!)
7 tbsp powdered sugar, 1 tsp vanilla essence

1. Mix ¼ cup water and 4 tbsp sugar in a pan. Stirring continuously, cook on low heat till sugar melts. Cook further for 2 minutes. Remove from fire. After it cools, add strawberries to the sugar syrup and stir gently for

Contd...

a few seconds till well coated and glazed. Remove the glazed strawberries to a plate with a slotted spoon, leaving the syrup behind in the pan.

2. For the soaking syrup, mix cornflour dissolved in water to the left over syrup of the strawberries in the pan. Cook, stirring continuously till it boils. Simmer for 1-2 minutes. Remove from fire. Add rum or brandy or essence. Mix. Keep aside.

3. Beat the cream in a chilled pan with lemon juice, powdered sugar and vanilla essence on ice till stiff peaks are formed. Fill cream for icing in an icing bag. Keep the left over cream and the icing bag in the fridge.

4. Cut the cake into 2 round halves. Spoon 3-4 tbsp syrup from the pan on each piece of cake. Keep one piece on a high platform that the cake is at eye level to get a neat finish. Spread 4-5 tbsp cream on each piece of the cake and sandwich the two pieces together. Keep the remaining cream for icing.

5. Top the cake with 2-3 tbsp cream and spread it thinly on the top.

6. Pipe icing on sides using the star nozzle, starting from bottom till the top edge to get straight thick lines which cover the sides completely.

7. Now pipe a lattice pattern (criss-cross) on the top, making squares big enough to accommodate a strawberry. (When you cross a line while piping, lift icing bag slightly to get beautiful curves!)
8. Arrange the strawberries in a ring inside the squares. Make a border of small rosettes of cream, by simply swirling the icing gun and then pulling it up and releasing pressure at the same time. Refrigerate till serving time.

For stars, hold the icing bag or gun at 90° angle with the tip slightly above the surface of the cake. Squeeze bag to form a star, then stop squeezing and pull bag away. The size of the star depends on the amount of pressure applied as well as the size of the opening of the bag. For a border, hold the bag at 45° angle and apply equal pressure as you move forward.

Whipped Cream Decoration

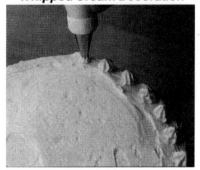

Orange Chiffon Cake with Orange Honey Sauce

Picture on page 66   *Serves* 12

ORANGE CHIFFON CAKE

1¾ cups maida (plain flour), 1½ tsp baking powder, ¾ tsp soda-bi-carb

¾ cup butter - softened, ¾ cup powdered sugar

¾ cup milk

6 tbsp orange squash - undiluted

ORANGE FILLING

¼ cup yellow butter, ½ cup icing sugar - sifted

1 tbsp orange rind, 1 tbsp orange squash

SAUCE

1 cup orange juice, 4 tbsp honey, 2 tbsp cornflour

OTHER INGREDIENTS
½ cup orange juice - to soak
some toasted almonds - cut into thin long pieces

1. For the cake, sieve the flour, baking powder and the soda-bi-carb.
2. Beat butter and sugar till light and fluffy. Add the milk and orange squash. Mix.
3. Add flour and beat well till fluffy. Pour into a cake tin of 8-9" diameter. Bake at 180°C/350°F for 25 minutes till golden and the cake shrinks from the sides of the tin. Let it cool before removing from the tin.
4. For the orange filling, take out orange rind by scraping the white pith beneath a 1" piece of orange peel by keeping it flat on a surface. Cut it very finely into thin strips.

Step 4

5. Beat butter and sugar till light and fluffy. Beat in the orange squash and rind.
6. Cut the cake into 2 round pieces. Place one piece on a big serving platter.

Contd...

7. Soak it with ¼ cup of orange juice. Spread the icing on it. Soak the other piece of cake and invert on the first piece of cake. Keep aside.

8. Toast 7-8 almonds in an oven for 10 minutes at 180°C or roast them in a kadhai. Cut them into thin long pieces.

9. Mix all ingredients of the sauce and cook till it attains a coating consistency.

Step 7

10. Prick cake lightly. Pour the hot sauce over the cake. Let it drizzle on the sides. Sprinkle toasted almonds. Serve.

Note: If you wish, you may make extra sauce and serve in a sauce boat or a bowl along with the cake.

Puddings & Pies

STEPS FOR MAKING A SHORT CRUST SHELL FOR HONEY & NUT PIE ...

A 9" flan tin with a loose (removable) bottom.

Press the rolled out dough into the flan tin.

To trim off the excess dough, simply roll a rolling pin over the edges of the flan tin. The rim will act as a cutting edge and the excess will fall away.

Nougat Date Pudding

Serves 6-8

PUDDING

½ tin milk-maid (condensed milk)
½ cup (80 gms) butter
250 gms dates
½ tsp soda-bi-carb
85 gms (a little more than ¾ cup) maida (plain flour)
1 tsp baking powder
½ cup walnuts, ½ tsp vanilla essence

TO SOAK

1 cup hot milk

CUSTARD SAUCE

2½ cups milk, 3 tbsp sugar
2½ tbsp custard powder
½ cup cream

PRALINE POWDER
3 tbsp almonds, 3 tbsp sugar

1. Remove seeds from dates and chop them.
2. Soak in 5 tbsp of water with ½ tsp of soda for 4-5 hours or overnight.
3. Sift maida with baking powder. Add dates and walnuts to the maida. Mix well.
4. Beat condensed milk and butter well, in a clean pan.
5. Add the maida mixture to the condensed milk mixture. Add essence and beat well.
6. Transfer the mixture to a greased oven proof glass serving dish. Bake in a pre-heated oven at 150°C for about 30 minutes. Check pudding with a knife before removing from the oven. Soak the pudding with 1 cup of hot milk immediately after removing from the oven. Keep aside (not in the fridge).
7. Prepare custard sauce by dissolving custard powder in ½ cup milk.
8. Heat the remaining 2 cups of milk with sugar. When it boils, add the custard powder, stirring continuously.

Contd...

9. Cook for a few minutes till it coats the back of the spoon. Keep aside to cool. Mix in cream. Keep aside.
10. For the praline powder, melt the sugar in a heavy bottom kadhai on very low heat till golden. Add the nuts and stir for a few seconds until rich brown in colour. Spread the mixture immediately on a greased rolling board (chakla). When cold, crush it with a rolling pin (belan) to a coarse powder. Keep aside.
11. To serve, heat the custard on low heat till it is about to boil. Remove from fire. Pour some over the pudding. Sprinkle the praline and serve with the left over custard put in a small bowl or a sauce boat.

Note: In summers, you need not heat the custard. You can whip chilled custard and pour on it.

Honey & Nut Pie

Honey flavoured dates & walnuts are baked on a short crust pastry shell. A loose bottomed flan tin of 9" diameter is ideal for making it.

Serves 10

SHORT CRUST PASTRY

200 gms (2 cups) flour (maida)
a small pinch of baking powder, 2 tbsp powder sugar
100 gms salted butter (cold and solid), 3-4 tbsp ice cold water to bind

FILLING

200 gm dates - deseeded, chopped finely and soaked in ½ cup water for 6-8
hours or overnight with a pinch of soda-bi-carb
2-3 apples - peeled and grated
½ cup water, 4 tbsp lemon juice, 6 tbsp honey
2 tbsp black raisins, ½ cup chopped walnuts

1. For the short crust pastry, cut cold butter into tiny cubes.
2. Sift flour with baking powder and sugar. In a blender put the flour

Contd...

mix. Add the butter and churn for a few seconds. Scrape the sides with a spatula or a knife and churn again for a few seconds only. Do not churn the mixer too much. Transfer to a mixing bowl. Mix lightly.

3. Add just enough ice cold water to form a dough. Wrap in a damp cloth and keep in the fridge for 15-20 minutes to get cold.

4. For the filling, mix all ingredients except walnuts. Heat on slow fire, for about 10 minutes, till pulpy and dry. Add half of the walnuts, keeping aside the rest for the topping. Remove from fire and keep aside.

5. For the pie, roll out pastry so that it is ¼" thick and 4" bigger in diameter than the flan tin or the pie dish, such that it covers the base and the sides of the tin or pie dish as shown on page 57. If you find it difficult to roll it fully, roll out a little and place it in the tin and spread it out with the fingers to cover the bottom & sides of the tin.

6. Prick base with a fork. Bake at 200°C in a pre-heated oven for 15 minutes or till the pastry shell turns light brown. Remove from oven.

7. Arrange dry filling over it. Level it. Sprinkle some walnuts on top. Keep aside till serving time. To serve, bake for 10-12 minutes in a pre-heated oven at 150°C. Serve hot with vanilla ice cream or fresh cream.

Bread Pudding

A crunchy bread pudding flavoured with orange marmalade

Serves 6-8

6 slices of brown bread - buttered nicely and spread with orange marmalade

MIX TOGETHER
6 tbsp kellogs cornflakes
3 tbsp melted butter, 2 tbsp powdered sugar

FILLING
4 pears or 2 apples - peeled and cut into four and then into thin slices
¼ tsp cinnamon (dalchini) powder
1 tsp lemon juice
2-3 tbsp kishmish (raisins) - soaked in water
2 tbsp brown sugar

CUSTARD
2 cups milk
2 tbsp sugar, 2 tbsp cornflour, 1 tsp vanilla essence

TOPPING
10-15 almonds - sliced
5-6 glace cherries - sliced thinly

1. Remove sides of bread and cut into thin long fingers.
2. Arrange fingers of 3 slices in a medium sized greased oven proof dish.
3. Sprinkle half the cornflakes mixed with butter and sugar over it.
4. Mix some lemon juice and dalchini powder to the fruit. Arrange half of the fruit slices and kishmish on the cornflakes.
5. Sprinkle some brown sugar on top.
6. Repeat the layer of bread fingers, cornflakes and the left over fruit and kishmish.
7. Dissolve cornflour in ¼ cup milk. Boil leftover milk with sugar. Add cornflour paste and cook till a thick custard of pouring consistency is ready. Add essence.
8. Pour the custard over the fruit.
9. Top with sliced almonds and glace cherries.
10. Bake in a moderate oven at 180°C for about 30 minutes or till golden. Serve hot.

Vanilla Choco Mousse : Recipe on page 80 ➢

Apple Crumble

Serves 8-10

TOPPING
2 cups flour (maida)
1 tsp baking powder
1 cup powdered sugar
½ cup butter

APPLE LAYER
8 apples (1½ kg) - peeled and cut into slices
½ cup sugar
2 tbsp lemon juice (juice of 1 lemon)
1 tsp powdered cinnamon (dalchini)

◁ *Orange Chiffon Cake with Orange Honey Sauce: Recipe on page 54*

1. Sieve the flour, baking powder and powdered sugar.
2. Cut the butter into small pieces.
3. Rub butter in the flour mix with your finger tips till the mixture resembles fine bread crumbs. Keep aside.
4. Peel and slice the apples. Add lemon juice.
5. Add ½ cup sugar and the cinnamon powder. Cook for 5 minutes till apples are slightly tender. Do not mash the slices.
6. Arrange the apple slices in a greased oven proof glass baking dish.
7. Spread the flour mixture over the apples. Press gently.
8. Bake in a pre-heated oven for 30-40 minutes or until slightly golden.
9. Serve with ice cream or whipped cream.

Mousses & Soufflés

Marble Grape Mousse

A stunning combination of black grape mousse and vanilla mousse.

Picture on page 1   *Serves 8*

1 tin milk-maid (condensed milk), 2 cups boiling hot water
1½ tsp vanilla essence
600 gms cream (3 packs of vijaya cream or 3½ cups fresh cream)
2 packets (20 gm) china grass
3-4 tbsp powdered sugar
2 tsp lemon juice
½ cup black grapes

COOK TOGETHER
250 gm black grapes, 1 cup water, 2 tbsp sugar

1. Cook grapes with 1 cup water and 2 tbsp sugar till it boils. Reduce heat and cook further for 10 minutes till soft. Remove from fire. Cool. Blend in a mixer. Strain if there are seeds. Keep aside.

2. Beat condensed milk with 2 cups hot boiling water and essence in a

big pan. Cover and keep aside.

3. Break china grass into pieces and add 2½ cups water to it. Leave for 5 minutes to swell. Heat on slow fire, stirring, till it dissolves completely.

4. Gradually add the hot melted china grass into the **hot condensed milk** mixture, stirring continuously with the other hand. Mix well.

5. Beat cream separately till slightly fluffy.

6. Add cream to the condensed milk and mix well till smooth. Check sugar. Add powdered sugar to taste.

7. Divide mixture into 2 equal parts. Keep one part plain as vanilla and add 2 tsp lemon juice to it and mix well. Keep aside in the fridge for about 30 minutes till almost set.

8. Add the left over mousse mix to the grape mixture and mix well to get grape mousse. Keep in the fridge for 30 minutes or more till the mixture is almost set.

9. Drop a spoonful of white mousse in a serving cup or glass, then 1 spoonful of grape mousse. Add 2-3 black grapes and then repeat both the mousses. Top with 2-3 grapes. Serve cold.

Pineapple Soufflé

Servings 8

½ tin condensed milk (milk-maid) at room temperature
1 small tin of pineapple slices - at room temperature, see note
1 packet of china grass (10 gm)
3 tsp lemon juice, ½ cup water
250 gms cream
1 tbsp powdered sugar for decoration
1½ tsp of pineapple essence, a few drops of yellow colour
a few glace cherries for decoration

1. Beat condensed milk till light and creamy. Keep aside.
2. Chop 2 slices of pineapples finely. Keep aside.
3. Take 1 cup pineapple syrup of the tin in a pan and add ½ cup water to it. Heat it on low heat till just about to boil. Cover and keep aside.
4. Break china grass into small pieces. Pour 1¼ cups water on it and keep aside to swell for 5 minutes. Stir continuously on low heat till it melts properly. Remove from fire.

5. Add the hot china grass solution into the **hot pineapple syrup** gradually, stirring well with the other hand.

6. Add the hot pineapple syrup with china grass into the milk-maid, stirring continuously.

7. Add the chopped pineapple pieces and 3 tsp lemon juice also to the condensed milk. Mix very well. Keep aside till it comes to room temperature and is no longer hot.

8. Beat 250 gm cream till slightly thick: Add 200 gms of cream to the condensed milk mixture keeping aside 50 gms for decoration.

9. Add essence and colour. Beat well till smooth.

10. Pour into a serving dish and refrigerate for 3-4 hours or till set.

11. Whip 50 gm cream with 1 tbsp powdered sugar till stiff peaks form. Decorate with glace cherries and whipped cream. Keep in the fridge till serving time.

Note: Store the leftover pineapples alongwith the syrup in a steel or plastic box in the freezer compartment of the refrigerator for 2-3 months without getting spoilt.

Chocolate Mousse

Serves 6

3 cups milk
3 tbsp cocoa powder
1½ tbsp cornflour
6 tbsp sugar
1 pack china grass (10 gm)
60 gm (1½ slabs) cadburys bournville chocolate - cut into small pieces
1 tsp coffee powder
1 tsp vanilla essence
1¼ cups (250 gm) cream - whipped till fluffy and slightly thick

DECORATION (OPTIONAL)
chocolate sprinklers or chocolate thins or nutties
100 gm cream - whipped till thick
chocolate sauce to coat

Chenna Kulfi: Recipe on page 91 ➤

1. Mix cocoa and cornflour in ½ cup milk in a small bowl to a paste.
2. Boil the rest of milk with sugar in a heavy bottomed pan.
3. Add cocoa and cornflour paste to the boiling milk, stirring continuously.
4. Add chocolate pieces. Cook on low heat for 3-4 minutes till chocolate dissolves. Add coffee and remove from fire. Cover and keep hot.
5. Break china grass into small pieces. Soak china grass in 1¼ cups water till it swells. Stir on low heat till it dissolves completely.
6. Add the china grass solution into the **hot chocolate custard**, stirring continuously. Let it cool down and become slightly thick.
7. Beat cream and essence till slightly thick and fluffy.
8. Add whipped cream to chocolate mixture. Beat well till smooth.
9. Coat the serving dish or individual cups with chocolate sauce.
10. Transfer the mixture in it. Refrigerate for 3-4 hours or till set.
11. Beat 100 gm cream with 2 tbsp powdered sugar and a drop of lemon juice till stiff peaks form. Put whipped cream in an icing bag. Keep in the freezer for 10 min. Decorate mousse with whipped cream and chocolate sprinklers or chocolate thins or nutties put on cream swirls.

◁ *Falooda : Recipe on page 90*

Mango Soufflé

Enjoy it even when mangoes are not in season!

Serves 10

2 packets (400 ml) mango fruity drink
8 tbsp sugar
1 packet china grass
1¼ cups water
250 gms cream
a few drops of yellow colour
1 mango - cut into tiny neat cubes or balls, if available, for decoration

1. In a clean pan mix mango fruity and sugar. Keep on fire and bring to a boil. Stir to dissolve sugar. Remove from fire. Cover and keep aside.
2. Break china grass into small pieces. Soak in 1¼ cups water for 5 minutes. Heat on slow fire to dissolve it completely.
3. Gradually add the hot china grass solution into the **hot fruity**, stirring continuously. Let it cool to room temperature & let it turn slightly thick.

4. Beat cream in a bowl till fluffy. Do not over beat the cream.
5. Beat the thickened fruity.
6. Add whipped cream and yellow colour. Beat well till smooth.
7. Transfer to a serving dish. Refrigerate for 2-3 hours till set.
8. Sprinkle very neatly cut mango pieces on the set dessert.
9. Keep in the fridge till serving time.
10. 15 minutes before serving, return to the freezer to chill it properly. Serve chilled.

Vanilla Choco Mousse

A stunning combination of chocolate and vanilla mousse. Topped with a halved cookie, it looks irresistible!

Picture on page 65   *Serves 6*

600 gms cream (3 packs of vijaya cream or 3½ cups fresh cream)
1 tin milk-maid (condensed milk), 4 tsp lemon juice
2 packets china grass, 1½ tsp vanilla essence
2 tbsp powdered sugar or to taste
2 tbsp cocoa mixed with ¼ cup water

TOPPING
a few chocolate chip biscuits or cookies

FOR COATING THE CUPS OR DISH OR GLASSES
2-3 tbsp chocolate sauce

1. Beat condensed milk till creamy. Add lemon juice and beat some more. Add 2½ cups boiling hot water and mix well. Cover and keep aside.
2. Break china grass into small pieces. Soak in 2½ cups water. Leave

for 5 minutes. Heat on slow fire, stirring, till it dissolves. Add the hot china grass solution into the **hot condensed milk mixture**, stirring continuously with the other hand. Add essence. Beat well on low speed for a few seconds. Keep aside for a few minutes, till slightly thick.

3. Beat the thickened condensed milk mixture till smooth.
4. Beat cream till slightly fluffy. Add cream to the above mixture and mix well till smooth. Add powdered sugar to taste.
5. Divide mixture into 2 equal parts. Keep one part plain as vanilla and keep aside in the fridge for about 30 minutes to set.
6. Mix cocoa with ¼ cup warm water in a pan. Stir on very low heat till a dark paste is ready. Remove from fire and let it cool down. Add the left over mousse mix in it and mix well to get chocolate mousse. Chill in the fridge for 30 minutes or more till the mixture is properly set.
7. Coat a dish or individual serving cups with chocolate sauce.
8. Drop a spoonful of white mousse, then 2 spoonfuls of chocolate mousse and finally a spoonful of white.
9. Keep in the fridge till serving time. To serve, decorate with crushed chocolate chip cookies or cookie halves.

Indian

Bread and Paneer Pudding

A very decorative & a delicious Indian bread pudding.

Serves 8-10

6 slices of bread - remove sides and deep fry till golden brown
5 tbsp of chopped mixed nuts (badam, kishmish, pista etc.)
¼ cup cold milk - to soak bread

PANEER LAYER
4 cups milk
½ cup sugar
¾ tsp powdered seeds of chhoti illaichi (green cardamom)
8 tsp cornflour dissolved in ½ cup milk
100 gms paneer - grated
2 drops of kewra essence or ½ tsp ruh kewra water

Step 1

1. For the paneer layer, boil 4 cups milk in a clean heavy bottomed kadhai. Simmer on low flame for 20 minutes.
2. In the meanwhile, boil ½ cup sugar with ½ cup water in a separate pan. Keep on low heat for 5 minutes. Add grated paneer. Cook for 1 minute. Remove from fire.
3. Add cornflour paste to the milk of step 1, stirring continuously. Keep stirring for 2 minutes till thick.
4. Add sugar and paneer mixture. Boil. Keep on heat for 1 minute. Remove from fire. Cool.

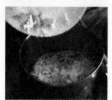

Step 2

5. Add essence. Sprinkle illaichi powder. Keep aside.
6. Remove the side crusts of bread. Heat oil in a kadhai. Deep fry each piece till golden brown. Let it cool.
7. Dip each piece of bread in some cold milk for a second. Remove immediately. Cut each slice into 4 square pieces. This way you get 24 small pieces of bread. *Contd...*

Purple Velvet Mousse: Recipe on page 93 ➤

8. Take a serving dish. Spread 1-2 tbsp of paneer mixture at the bottom of the dish. Place 8 pieces of fried bread (bread of 2 slices) joined together in a single layer at the base of the dish.

9. Spread about 1 tsp of the paneer mixture on each piece. Sprinkle 1 tbsp of chopped mixed nuts on the paneer.

Step 10

10. Repeat the bread layer in the same way with bread pieces first and then the paneer layer.

11. Top with 1½ tbsp of chopped mixed nuts.

12. Repeat with the left over bread, paneer and nuts to get a 3 layered pudding.

13. Cover with a cling wrap (plastic film) and let it set for atleast 1 hour before serving. Serve at room temperature.

◁ *Devil's Chocolate Mousse: Recipe on page 96*

Stuffed Khubani in Syrup

Picture on backcover   *Serves 8-10*

13 large dried imported seedless khubani (dried apricots, orange in colour)
some rose petals, to garnish

FILLING
50 gms paneer - grated very finely, seeds of 3 chhoti illaichi - powdered
5-6 badaam (almonds) - crushed coarsely, a drop of kewra essence

SYRUP
½ cup of sugar, 1 cup of water, 2-3 chhoti illaichi (green cardamoms)
2 drops of kewra essence

1. Take a khubani, make a small slit at one side of the khubani.

2. Insert the knife straight inside without puncturing any side. Rotate the knife gently, creating space for filling. Let the other end be intact. Do not puncture it, otherwise the

Step 1

filling will come out.
3. For the filling, grate paneer very finely. Add powdered illaichi seeds, crushed baadam and kewra essence. Mix gently.
4. For the syrup, heat sugar, water and illaichi together in a pan. Give 2- 3 boils. Cook on low heat for 3-4 minutes. Add essence.
5. Add khubani to the syrup and let it cook for another 2-3 minutes. Remove from fire. Let the khubanis cool in the syrup.
6. Take one piece of khubani at a time. Fill atleast ½ tsp of the paneer filling in each piece. Push gently.
7. Put back in the syrup. Keep in the fridge for atleast 2-3 hours before serving for the dessert to taste good.
8. At serving time, garnish with rose petals. Serve at room temperature.

Step 2

Step 6

Step 7

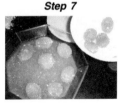

Falooda

Enjoy it as a drink or a dessert. Very popular on the beach side in Mumbai.

Picture on page 76   *Serves 6*

6 tbsp rice sewian or rice noodles - broken into short lengths, 1" pieces
2 tbsp subzah (basil) seeds or tookmalanga (black oval seeds which when
soaked develop a greyish, translucent, slippery coat), 4 cups milk, 2 tbsp sugar
9 tbsp rose syrup, 6 scoops vanilla ice cream

1. Soak the subzah seeds in 1 cup milk. Chill the seeds in milk for about 30 minutes or even more till they swell.
2. Boil the rice seviyaan or rice noodles in water for about 5 min until soft. Drain and refresh in cold water. Keep covered in the refrigerator.
3. Add 2 tbsp sugar to the remaining 3 cups milk. Keep in the fridge.
4. To serve, mix the milk with subzah seeds and whip well to mix the seeds. Divide it into 6 glasses. Add 1 tbsp noodles in each glass.
5. Then gently pour in the rose syrup which being heavier will settle to the bottom. Float a scoop of ice cream on top. Mix gently. Serve.

Chenna Kulfi

The khoya is substituted with low fat paneer.

Serves 15   *Picture on page 75*

1 kg (5 cups) milk - at room temperature
½ cup sugar
75 gm paneer - grated finely (¾ cup)
2 tbsp cornflour
seeds of 3-4 chhoti illaichi (green cardamoms) - crushed
1 tbsp kishmish (raisins), 1 tbsp shredded badam (almonds)

1. Dissolve cornflour in ¼ cup milk.
2. Heat the rest of the milk with sugar. Boil and keep on fire for about 20 minutes, till reduced to half the quantity. Add crushed illaichi seeds.
3. Add the cornflour paste to the boiling milk, stirring continuously.
4. Continue boiling, by lowering the flame, for about 2-3 minutes. Cool.
5. Add paneer, kishmish and almonds. Check sugar. Remove from fire.
6. Fill in clean kulfi moulds and leave to set in the freezer for 6-8 hours.

Low Calorie Desserts

Purple Velvet Mousse

An eye pleasing dessert. Hung curd is substituted for the rich cream.

Serves 6-8   *Picture on page 85*

½ tin milkmaid (condensed milk)
1 packet china grass (10 gm)
2½ cups black grapes (250 gm)
3 tbsp sugar
4 cups curd - hang in a muslin cloth for 30 minutes
a few drops of vanilla essence
a few drops of cochineal (strawberry red) colour

GLAZE (OPTIONAL)
½ cup black grapes
2 tbsp sugar
1 tbsp cornflour dissolved in ¼ cup water
¼ tsp butter

1. Hang curd in a muslin cloth for ½ hour. Squeeze gently to extract excess whey.
2. Cut ½ cup remaining grapes into 2 pieces. Deseed if it has seeds.
3. Cook 2 cups grapes with 1 cup water and 3 tbsp sugar. Boil. Simmer on low heat for 10 minutes till they turn soft. Remove from fire. Cool. Blend in a mixer to a puree. Strain the juice if there are seeds. Discard the residue. Heat the grape puree and cover and keep aside.
4. Break china grass into small pieces. Pour 1¼ cups of water over china grass in a pan. Keep aside to swell for 5 minutes. Keep on low heat till it dissolves completely. Remove from fire and add hot solution into hot grape puree. Keep aside.
5. Beat the condensed milk in a pan till creamy.
6. Add the china grass-grape puree to the condensed milk, and beat well till smooth.
7. Beat the curd with vanilla essence till smooth.
8. Add the curd to the grape and condensed milk mixture. Beat well. Add chopped grapes.

9. Transfer to a serving dish or individual mousse cups. Keep in the fridge for 3-4 hours or till set.
10. For the glaze, cook ½ cup grapes with 1 cup water and 2 tbsp sugar in a clean pan. Boil. Mash and cook till pulpy for about 3-5 minutes.
11. Remove from fire and strain. Measure in a cup. Add more water if required to make it to a full cup of grape juice.
12. Add 1 tbsp cornflour dissolved in ¼ cup water to grape juice. Cook grape juice, stirring, on low heat till slightly thick. Add butter. Remove from fire. Add a drop of strawberry red colour if you wish.
13. When glaze no longer remains hot, pour over the set dessert. Arrange a grape on top. Refrigerate till the time of serving.

Devil's Chocolate Mousse

Cream has been substituted with yogurt to make a delicious mousse!

Picture on page 86   *Serves 4*

2½ cups milk
2 tbsp cornflour
3 tbsp cocoa
18 tablets of artificial sweetner or 10 tbsp sugar, or to taste
½ tsp butter
1 packet china grass (10 gm)
2 cups thick curd - hang for ½ hour in a muslin cloth and squeeze well to
remove all whey
1½ tsp vanilla essence
2 tsp chocolate sauce and mint to garnish

1. Dissolve cornflour in ½ cup warm milk.
2. Put cocoa in a heavy bottomed pan. Pour ½ cup water on it and mix.
    Keep on fire and stir continuously on low heat, for about 2 minutes till
    a dark paste is ready. Remove from fire.

3. Add the rest of the milk to cocoa paste and mix well using a wire whisk. Mix the cocoa sticking on the sides of the pan nicely with the milk.
4. Keep on fire. When it starts boiling, add the dissolved cornflour paste, stirring continuously. Cook, stirring till the milk turns slightly thick, like custard and coats the spoon. Remove from fire. Cover and keep aside.
5. Break china grass into small pieces. Put in a pan and pour 1¼ cups water on it. Keep aside for 5 minutes to swell. Stir on low flame till china grass dissolves completely. Remove from fire and add hot china grass into the hot chocolate custard.
6. Mix in butter and artificial sweetner or sugar. Check sweetness. Keep chocolate custard aside. Let it cool down to room temperature.
7. Whip the hung curd with a whisk till smooth. Add essence also.
8. Add the curd mix to the chocolate custard and mix well.
9. Check sugar. Add 1-2 tbsp powdered sugar if required, depending on the sourness of the curd. Transfer to individual serving cups or a dish and keep in the fridge for 3-4 hours or till set.
10. Garnish with mint and a swirl of chocolate sauce.

Bread Cake Trifle

Serves 4-6

CHOCOLATE BREAD CAKE LAYER
4 slices bread
2 tbsp cocoa powder
3 tbsp walnuts (akhrot)
6 tablets artificial sweetner - powdered or 3 tbsp powdered sugar

CUSTARD LAYER
2½ cups (500 ml) milk
3 tbsp milk powder (skimmed)
12 tablets artificial sweetner or 4 tbsp sugar
2½ tbsp custard powder
1 tsp vanilla essence

DECORATIVE FRUIT TOPPING
¼ cup melon balls, ¼ cups watermelon balls
¼ cup mango balls or a few lychees, cherries or grapes
a few mint sprigs

1. Remove the side crust from bread slices and tear roughly.
2. Place bread pieces, cocoa, powdered sweetner or sugar and walnuts in a mixer grinder and blend to get smooth crumbs.
3. Place half the crumbs at the bottom of a small serving dish and press a little. Keep the remaining half of the crumbs aside.
4. For the custard layer, mix custard powder in ½ cup cold milk.
5. Mix milk powder to the remaining milk in a heavy bottom pan. Bring to a boil. Add the dissolved custard mixture. Cook, stirring, for 2-3 minutes on low heat. Remove from heat. Mix in sweetner or sugar.
6. Let the custard cool down and then add the vanilla essence.
7. Pour 4-5 tbsp custard over the bread crumbs placed in the serving dish. Cool the dessert in the fridge for 10 minutes to set.
8. When bread crumbs set, pour half of the remaining custard over the crumbs. Sprinkle the remaining crumbs. Finally pour the left over custard. Refrigerate till set.
9. Using a small scooper make balls of fruits or use cherries or grapes instead. Keep fruits in the fridge till serving time. Just before serving, arrange fruit over the pudding. Decorate with mint sprigs.

Pina Orange Dome Cake

Picture on page 103   *Serves 12*

CAKE

½ tin (200 gm) condensed milk (milk-maid)
¾ cup (150 ml) milk
¾ cup (90 gm) white butter
1½ tbsp powdered sugar
125 gms (1¼ cups) maida (plain flour)
½ tsp level soda-bi-carb, 1 tsp level baking powder
1 tsp vanilla essence
¼ tsp ground nutmeg (jaiphal)
2 tbsp orange rind (see step 8)

OTHER INGREDIENTS

1 cup orange juice - to soak cake
1 cup very finely chopped fresh ripe pineapple
1 orange - to decorate, separate segments and cut each into half lengthwise

FRESH PINEAPPLE TOPPING

4 cups chopped fresh ripe pineapple - blend to a puree in a mixer, 5 tbsp sugar
1 cup finely grated paneer (100 gm)
3 cups curd - hang for 30 minutes, 4 tbsp powdered sugar, or to taste

1. Preheat oven to 150°C for 10 minutes.
2. Sift maida with soda-bi-carb and baking powder. Keep aside.
3. Mix sugar and butter in a big pan. Beat till very fluffy and light.
4. Add milk-maid. Beat well to mix.
5. Add milk. Mix well. Add essence.
6. Add the maida gradually beating well after each addition.
7. Beat well for 3-4 minutes till the mixture is smooth and light and of a soft dropping consistency.

Step 8

8. To take out orange rind, keep a 2" peel of the orange on a surface, scrape the white pith below the skin with a knife and cut rind into thread thin pieces.
9. Mix in orange rind and nutmeg. Beat well.

Contd...

10. Spoon batter into an 10" dome shaped borosil glass bowl, greased with oil. Bake in a preheated 160°C oven for about 30 minutes.
11. Invert the cake to get the dome top. If the cake does not sit flat, cut a thin layer from the bottom. Cut the cake into 2 pieces horizontally.
12. Pour orange juice on both pieces to moisten the cake very nicely.
13. For the pineapple topping, cook pineapple puree with sugar till it boils. Simmer on low heat for 4-5 minutes. Remove from fire and let it cool.
14. Blend paneer in the mixer with half the pineapple puree till very smooth. Remove from blender. Add the left over pineapple puree and the hung curd. Beat to mix well. Add some powdered sugar as needed.
15. Spread 2 tbsp topping on one piece of the cake placed on the serving platter. Spread finely chopped pineapple. Spread some topping on the other piece of cake and invert it on the first piece. Press.
16. Pour the left over topping on the cake gradually, letting it pour down and covering the whole of the cake. Spread neatly with a knife. Arrange halved orange segments and whole almonds at the bottom.

Pina Orange Dome Cake: Recipe on page 100 ➤

BEST SELLERS BY *Nita Mehta*

LOW FAT Tasty Recipes

CHAAWAL

Dinner Menus
from around the world

MORE DESSERTS

PRESSURE COOKING

OVEN Recipes

Taste of RAJASTHAN

The Best of MUTTON

MORE CHICKEN

Great Ideas - Cooking Tips

LOSE WEIGHT

SANDWICHES